UNDERSTANDING THE PARANORMAL

INVESTIGATING MIRACLES

LEWIS M. STEINBERG

Britannica
Educational Publishing
IN ASSOCIATION WITH

ROSEN
EDUCATIONAL SERVICES

Published in 2017 by Britannica Educational Publishing (a trademark of Encyclopædia Britannica, Inc.) in association with The Rosen Publishing Group, Inc.
29 East 21st Street, New York, NY 10010

Distributed exclusively by Rosen Publishing.
To see additional Britannica Educational Publishing titles, go to rosenpublishing.com.

First Edition

Britannica Educational Publishing
J.E. Luebering: Executive Director, Core Editorial
Anthony L. Green: Editor, Compton's by Britannica

Rosen Publishing
Jacob R. Steinberg: Editor
Nelson Sá: Art Director
Brian Garvey: Designer
Cindy Reiman: Photography Manager
Bruce Donnola: Photo Researcher

Library of Congress Cataloging-in-Publication Data

Names: Steinberg, Lewis M., author.
Title: Investigating miracles / Lewis M. Steinberg.
Description: First Edition. | New York : Britannica Educational Publishing, 2017. | Series: Understanding the paranormal | Includes bibliographical references and index.
Identifiers: LCCN 2015045144| ISBN 9781508102236 (library bound : alk. paper) | ISBN 9781680485776 (pbk. : alk. paper) | ISBN 9781680485547 (6-pack : alk. paper)
Subjects: LCSH: Supernatural—Juvenile literature. | Miracles—Juvenile literature.
Classification: LCC BL100 .S44 2016 | DDC 202/.117—dc23
LC record available at http://lccn.loc.gov/2015045144

Manufactured in the United States of America

Photo credits: Cover, p. 1 Rocksweeper/Shutterstock.com; pp. 5, 20 British Library, London, UK/Bridgeman Images; pp. 7, 19 © Chronicle/Alamy Stock Photo; p. 8 © PhotoStock-Israel/Alamy Stock Photo; p. 10 © AP Images; p. 12 Private Collection/The Stapleton Collection/Bridgeman Images; p. 14 © Pictures From History/The Image Works; p. 18 DEA Picture Library/De Agostini/Getty Images; p. 21 Print Collector/Hulton Archive/Getty Images; p. 22 State Hermitage Museum, St. Petersburg, Russia/Bridgeman Images; p. 26 Photos.com/Thinkstock; p. 27 Godong/robertharding/Getty Images; p. 28 © Painting/Alamy Stock Photo; p. 32 Michel Baret/Gamma-Rapho/Getty Image; p. 34 Archivo Capitular de la Real Colegiata de San Isidoro, Leon, Spain/Bridgeman Images; pp. 35, 37 Heritage Images/Hulton Fine Art Collection/Getty Images; p. 39 courtesy Everett Collection; p. 40 John Olson/The LIFE Picture Collection/Getty Images; interior pages backgrounds © iStockphoto.com/Kivilvim Pinar, © iStockphoto.com/mitja2.

CONTENTS

INTRODUCTION

Many people use the word "miracle" in everyday life. In fact, we often hear and use such phrases as, "It's a miracle!" or that somebody is "hoping for a miracle." But many of the events we call miracles are simply unexpected or just a matter of luck. In their true sense, miracles are extraordinary happenings that do not follow the laws of nature. Because they cannot be explained rationally, people believe miracles occur at the hands of a divine power or force. Humans have written about miracles throughout most of history. Quite often unexplainable events have, at first, been called miracles. However, many of these so-called miracles were later found to be explainable through science. Other miracles have simply been legends, told to encourage faith in a divine figure or a god.

Miracles have a long history and have been a part of many diverse cultures. Today, science has given us a greater understanding of how nature works. As a result, we now know the causes for previously unexplained events. Still, believers often attribute positive outcomes to divine intervention. By investigating what believers say about miracles—and the science that explains many of them—we can better understand this spiritual phenomenon that holds a special place in so many cultures.

St. Cuthbert Healing a Child with the Plague, *illustration from the prose work* Life of St. Cuthbert *composed by Saint Bede the Venerable (written some time before 721).*

CHAPTER ONE

WHAT IS A MIRACLE?

People regularly refer to an uncommon event with a positive outcome as a miracle. The term originally comes from the Latin word *miraculum*, a sight that causes wonder and astonishment because of how extraordinary it is. Today, the word "miracle" generally refers to an event whose occurrence cannot be explained by normal standards or human understanding of the laws of nature.

Occurrences that initially appear to meet this standard may later be found to have an explanation. As science develops, previously unexplainable phenomena become understood. Because of this, some miracles are later disproven. Nevertheless miracles hold an important place in many religions and cultures. And despite scientific evidence to the contrary, believers often insist on the miraculous nature of certain events.

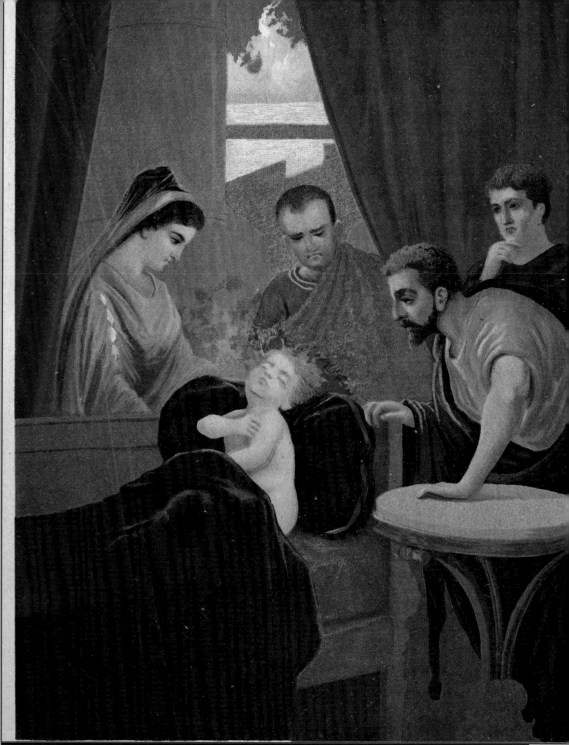

In Latin the word miraculum *described any scene that caused wonder. The Roman historian Livy used the word to describe an episode from Roman king Servius Tullius's childhood in which the future king's head burst into flames as he slept and he lay undisturbed.*

DEFINING MIRACLES

In almost all religious traditions, a miracle is an extraordinary and astonishing happening attributed to the action of a divine power. A miracle, therefore, is not just an amazing act; it also serves as a sign of the intervention of a higher being. Depending on the religion, the higher being may be God or angels. At times, miracles are performed through holy persons or

Believers often visit holy sites or the graves of saints to ask for miracles. Many Jews, for example, visit the tomb of Rabbi Meïr Ba'al ha-Nes (also known as Rabbi Meïr the Miracle Worker) in Tiberius, Israel, to ask for divine help.

sacred objects and places. Belief in miracles is a feature of most religions. For believers, the importance of miracles comes from the acceptance that they are signs of divine intervention.

Other than their defiance of natural laws and the belief that they are the result of divine intervention, there is no precise rule that defines an event as a miracle. The classification often depends on subjective standards. Those who deny the existence of higher beings generally outright deny the occurrence of miracles. For them, unexplained phenomena are attributable to a lack of scientific understanding—not a higher being.

Even among believers, most people would not consider a wholly internal experience or vision to be a miracle. Miracles are taken as outer, objective events. Throughout history, figures seeking to enhance their power or influence at times used deception, tricking believers into thinking a miracle had occurred.

PURPOSE OF MIRACLES

Miracles can serve many purposes. Ultimately they enhance religious followers' belief in the power to which they are attributed. They serve as proof—albeit unscientific—that a higher being (such as God) exists

Weeping statues are sometimes taken by Roman Catholic believers to be miracles. This Madonna statue in Civitavecchia, Italy, was claimed by believers to cry blood; however, forensic testing found that the blood belonged to a male human. The tears had been a hoax.

and guides or protects believers. A miracle may also validate the holiness of a person (such as wonder-working saints), a site (such as a holy shrine or a saint's tomb), or an object (such as relics or holy images).

The purpose of some miracles is shown in the immediate and direct result of the event. This result may be deliverance from danger, cure of illness, or the

MIRACLES IN EASTERN RELIGIONS

In the religions of the East, such as Hinduism and Buddhism, miracles are tied to the idea that those who practice self-discipline and become spiritually advanced can gain magical powers. Any holy person can gain such miraculous powers. According to the teaching of the Buddha, there are three kinds of miracles: the miracle of magic, the miracle of thought reading, and the miracle of instruction. The Buddha himself, however, refused to spread his teaching by impressing his audience with miracles. In China, the philosophical and religious tradition of Daoism has produced popular folk belief in miracle working and magic.

provision of plenty to the needy. These types of miracles are found throughout the Hebrew Bible. Notable miracles were the splitting of the Red Sea, by which the Israelites escaped Egypt, and the manna, a form of nourishment that miraculously appeared in the desert to feed the Israelites.

This illustration from the Nuremberg Bible depicts the miraculous provision of manna to the Israelites in the desert as described in the Hebrew Bible.

FAITH HEALING

Faith healing is the use of prayer and touch to treat physical or mental illnesses. It is a form of folk medicine. Faith healing is thought by believers to awaken divine power and provide miraculous recovery from disease or disability. However, by nonbelievers, faith healers are generally assumed to be frauds. If legitimate healing does occur, nonbelievers often attribute it to unknown (but scientific) reasons.

Most faith healers and other practitioners of folk medicine use some combination of prayer, charms, laying on of hands, and rubbing or massaging. They may also prescribe herbal teas or concoctions of animal parts and vegetables.

Faith healing has been associated with the miracle cures performed by Jesus in the New Testament. The practice also has a long history in the many instances of healing attributed to Christian saints. Many modern so-called faith healers, a popular fixture in evangelical Christianity and the New Age Movement, have been shown to use techniques of stage magic and other deception to give the appearance of divine power.

In the New Testament Jesus worked many miracles. Jesus is reported in the Gospels to have performed miracles of diverse kinds: raising the dead, healing the sick, casting out demons, and causing nature miracles, such as the multiplication of loaves and the turning of water into wine at the town of Cana. These miracles served as a sign of Jesus's role as messiah. Jesus repeatedly credited his faith as the source of these works.

An 18th-century illuminated manuscript from the Ottoman Empire depicts Buraq, the mythical horse on which the Prophet Muhammad miraculously traveled from Mecca to Jerusalem in a single night.

Given that Islam builds upon Christian and Jewish traditions and accepts the Hebrew Bible and the New Testament as holy (albeit corrupted) texts, Muslims believe in and accept the miracles of the Exodus narrative and of Jesus. Nevertheless, the Prophet Muhammad rejected the need to prove his own calling through miracles. Muslims believe that the writing of the Koran itself was the greatest miracle. Yet certain miracles are ascribed to Muhammad in the Koran. These include Muhammad's myriad prophecies, the splitting of the moon (Koran, chapter 54), and Muhammad's journey from Mecca to Jerusalem (and then heaven) in a single night (Koran, chapter 17).

CHAPTER TWO

THE HISTORY OF MIRACLES

I n many early civilizations, the operation of extra-ordinary forces was taken for granted. Therefore, events that later cultures would deem miraculous simply formed part of the total world picture. Magic, oracles, divination, and shamanism were all parts of ordinary life. This holds true for both nonurban cultures and more highly developed ones (such as the ancient classical and Oriental civilizations). Divine or spiritual actions were often considered to be a part of the normal order of things. As higher forms of religion developed, so did the concept of miracles—the intervention of divine forces in an otherwise ordered, physical world.

IN ANCIENT GREECE AND ROME

One early civilization in which miracles played a major part is that of ancient Greece. The intervention of the gods in the affairs of the Homeric heroes takes place in a world in which the divine and human spheres still interact. Later Greek religion and philosophy regarded our earthly world as distinct from the divine realm, though higher powers could still intervene in it. Miraculous cures, divine manifestations of various kinds (such as voices and in dreams), and even virgin births and resurrections were widely reported.

Asclepius, the Greek god of medicine, became associated with miraculous healing. Because it was thought that he cured the sick through dreams, the practice of sleeping in his temples in Epidaurus in southern Greece became common. In 293 BCE his cult spread to Rome, where he was worshiped as Aesculapius. The hero Heracles, too, was associated with miraculous healing.

In the Roman world miracles became increasingly associated with human figures. Apollonius of Tyana (flourished 1st century CE, Tyana, Cappadocia) was a pagan mystic who became a mythical hero during the time of the Roman Empire. An official biography of Apollonius portrays a figure much like Jesus in temperament and

This illustration shows a reconstruction of how the temple of the Greek god Asclepius in Epidaurus, Greece, may have appeared. It was a common practice for the ill to sleep in his temple, hoping to be cured by Asclepius through dreams.

power and claims that Apollonius performed certain miracles. Many pagans in the Roman Empire believed what was said in this work, and it inspired religious feeling in many of them. To honor and worship Apollonius, they erected shrines and other memorials. Roman emperor Vespasian (9–79 CE; ruled 69–79 CE) was another figure rumored to be able to heal the sick.

As philosophy and science grew in importance in the Greco-Roman world, skepticism toward belief in miracles increased. Miracle stories came to be seen as just that—stories.

MIRACLES OF THE HEBREW BIBLE

Miracles are taken for granted throughout the Hebrew Bible. God does "wondrous things" according to Psalms, chapter 72. Such wondrous things include acts of creation in general and in the history of the Israelites in particular. God's miracles range from routine interruptions of nature to tales of extraordinary intervention.

Apollonius Tÿanæus

nfpexi fecreta Deúm: et conceſſa faculta Naturæ exacta cognitione frui.

Apollonius of Tyana was a pagan mystic who lived during the 1st century CE. After an official biography promoted his miracle-working abilities, Apollonius was honored and worshipped as a Roman pagan alternative to the figure of Jesus.

One of the greatest miracles in Judaism is the creation of the world itself, as related in the biblical book of Genesis. In subsequent

Several of the 10 plagues of Egypt are illustrated in the Golden Haggadah, produced in Barcelona in 1320. In the Hebrew Bible it is narrated that God intervened on behalf of the Israelites by casting 10 plagues on their Egyptian captors.

books of the Bible, miracles of the saving kind become common. It is written that God miraculously inflicted the 10 plagues on Egypt, allowing the Israelites to escape slavery. When the Israelites' path was blocked by the waters of the Red Sea, it is written that through Moses, God caused the waters to separate long enough for the Israelites to escape, yet released them in time to drown the Egyptian pursuers. As the Israelites spent 40 years in the desert during their return to the so-called Promised Land, several miracles occurred, including the provision of food and water.

Later Judaism would show less interest in miracles, accepting those narrated in the Bible but directing focus instead on doing God's will.

IN CHRISTIANITY

Christianity was born in the Roman Empire in the 1st century CE. Its beliefs and practices are based on the teachings of Jesus Christ (*c.* 6–4 BCE–*c.* 30 CE). The new religion and its earliest believers emerged from Judaism, which had spread from its homeland in Judaea throughout the entire Roman Empire. The religion of the Jews provided important texts (the Hebrew Bible, or what Christians call the Old Testament) for the first Christians.

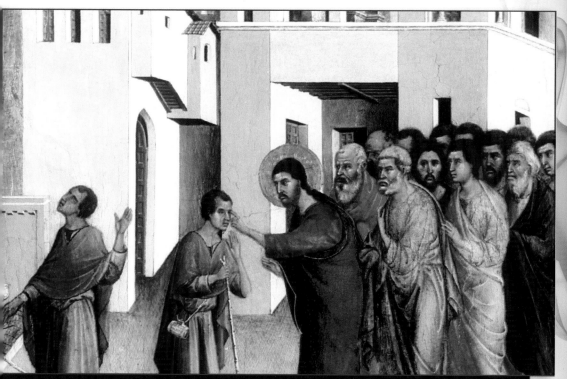

Jesus Opens the Eyes of the Man Born Blind, *tempera on panel, by Duccio di Buon-insegna, 1311. Many miracles, including several of the healing kind, were attributed to Jesus Christ in the New Testament.*

The New Testament accounts for the major events in the life of Jesus. It is written that Jesus performed many miracles. These include healing the sick, providing food when needed by multiplying loaves of bread, and turning water into wine. It is also written that Jesus raised the dead, as in the well-known story of Lazarus, a man who was brought back to life by Jesus four days after the man's death. Belief in Jesus—and in his miraculous deeds—is central to most Christian doctrine.

Early Christianity developed in Greco-Roman culture, which was full of miraculous accounts and legends. Whereas for early Christian theologians, miracles were a sign of the saving presence and design of God, many believers saw them as a sacred power manifested in individual persons, places, and objects.

This Byzantine icon depicts Saint Gregory Thaumaturgus (also known as Saint Gregory the Wonderworker). In Christianity, the performance of miracles is a requirement for elevation to sainthood, and many believers attribute miracles to venerated saints.

Medieval theologians taught that although knowledge was derived from facts, a certain amount of supernatural knowledge could be gained through miracles. Christianity assumes a natural order exists in the universe. However, as creator of that order, God can temporarily suspend it and perform miracles. Belief in miracles is obligatory in the Roman Catholic Church (although belief in any specific miracle is not). In Roman Catholic belief, miracles are often attributed to saints—either in person or the saint's tomb or relics. Protestantism only believes in the miracles written about in the Bible.

IN ISLAM

Muslims believe that Allah has worked miracles in the past (as through Jesus, for example). However, the Prophet Muhammad called himself a human messenger and preacher of repentance and rejected the idea of performing miracles. Despite this, Muslims believe the revelation of the Koran through Muhammad is the greatest miracle.

Later Muslim popular belief abounds in miracle stories and wonder-working saints. However, unlike Christianity or Judaism, Islam does not assume nature to operate according to fixed laws. The regularity of nature is viewed as the regularity of Allah's habit of recreating the universe through time, and a miracle is the

RELICS

Relics are the mortal remains of a saint. In a broader sense, a relic may also be an object that has been in contact with the saint. Among the major religions, Christianity (almost exclusively in Roman Catholicism) and Buddhism have emphasized the veneration of relics.

The basis of Christian belief in relics is the idea that reverence for the relics adds to the honor of the saint. In turn, miracles are often attributed to the divine powers of relics or the shrines of such saints. The first Christian reference to relics comes from Acts of the Apostles and explains that handkerchiefs that touched the skin of St. Paul were able to heal the sick and exorcise demons. The veneration of relics continued to grow in Christianity. Generally, the expectation of miracles increased during the Middle Ages. St. Thomas Aquinas (1224–1274), the great Roman Catholic theologian, considered it natural to worship the remains of saints. He further justified such worship by citing the miracles God worked in the presence of relics.

omnipotent God's departure from the usual course of things. Though miracles loom large in popular Muslim belief, generally speaking, they do not play a role in the continued life of orthodox Islam.

CHAPTER THREE

EXPLAINING MIRACLES

Miracles are only ever considered as such by believers. Nonbelievers generally fall into one of two groups: those who believe that science has—or eventually will—explain the reason for the occurrence and others who feel that the miracle was the result of deception or misunderstanding. The fact that an event has no current scientific explanation does not mean that it never will. As our understanding of the laws of nature expands, so does our understanding of causality.

IN CLASSICAL ANTIQUITY

Miracles were denied even in classic antiquity. The Roman statesman Cicero (106–43 BCE) wrote, "Nothing happens without a cause, and nothing happens unless it can

Cicero was a Roman statesman, scholar, and writer who, in his De divinatione *("On Divination") denied the existence of miracles.*

happen. When that which can happen does, in fact, happen, it cannot be considered a miracle. Hence there are no miracles." Cicero maintained that once an event has occurred, it couldn't be considered a miracle. Its very occurrence negates its miraculous nature. Cicero also said, however, that miracle stories may be necessary for the spiritual beliefs of ignorant folk.

Much of the debate in classical antiquity did not seek to deny the existence of miracles as such but rather to disprove those accepted by an opposing belief. While the existence of Jesus is historically documented, many of his miraculous works are the source of much speculation. Devout Christians accept the miracles performed by Jesus and other early figures of Christianity. However, Jews and Roman pagans of the time disputed the miracles discussed in the New Testament. The Talmud (a Jewish collection of legal commentary) attributes Jesus's miracles to "sorcery" and "magic." The 2nd-century Roman philosopher Celsus declared that Christian miracles were most improbable. If they had occurred, he insisted they were no match for the miracles of the pagan gods (such as Asclepius).

Shown is a set of the Jewish legal commentary known as the Talmud, in which early Jewish rabbis attributed the miracles of Jesus Christ to "sorcery" and "magic."

IN THE 18TH AND 19TH CENTURIES

The 18th-century Scottish philosopher David Hume was a leading rationalist who highly doubted the existence of true miracles. Hume devoted a full chapter of An Enquiry Concerning Human Understanding to a discussion of miracles.

Rationalist thought had existed since the Middle Ages. However, in the 18th and 19th centuries, it became a major factor. Rationalists believe that reason should be the basis for religious truth. David Hume was an 18th-century philosopher who tried to describe how the mind works to acquire knowledge. Hume dedicated an entire chapter of his book *An Enquiry Concerning Human Understanding* to the subject of miracles. He believed that there could be no knowledge of anything beyond experience. Because our experience of nature is so uniform, Hume concluded that miracles were highly unlikely.

Because they all agreed that prophecies and miracles were fundamental parts of their religion, Christians of the era devoted a good deal of writing to defending their faith

EMPIRICISM AND RATIONALISM

In the Enlightenment era of the 17th and 18th centuries, philosophers took interest in the nature of the human mind and its abilities to master the natural world. The two main philosophical points of view were empiricism and rationalism.

Empiricism holds that all knowledge comes from, and must be tested by, sensory experience. Early in the modern period Francis Bacon of England was the leading voice of empiricism. Later, leading empiricists included Thomas Hobbes, John Locke, George Berkeley, and David Hume. These philosophers were concerned with how the mind can know. Hume carried empiricism to its ultimate conclusion in his radical skepticism, contending no reality beyond perception can ever be proved. Rationalism regards reason as the ultimate source of human knowledge. Modern rationalism originated in the work of French philosopher René Descartes.

on the basis of the miracles recorded in the Bible. Meanwhile, advancements in science were proving just how complex and vast natural law truly was. This was enough wonderment for the rationalists. They typically viewed Christians as superstitious.

With the rise of rationalism, miracles were challenged in many fields. From the perspectives of philosophy and science, miracles were impossible or, at least, could not be proven within the limits of knowledge. Such a belief held that past "miracles" simply had yet to be explained by science. In the fields of history and literary criticism, the argument arose that the occurrence of past miracles was unproven. Nevertheless, an interest emerged in the growth and changes in legends and texts that reported miracles. In the field of psychology, arguments developed that some people want to believe in miracles, and so they produce imaginative creations to meet their own religious needs. Even some religious criticism suggested that a truly spiritual person did not need to believe in miracles to support his or her faith. Also emerging was the belief that the term "miracle" should not describe an objective event but rather a subjective mode of experience.

IN THE LATE 19TH AND 20TH CENTURIES

In the late 19th and 20th centuries, some liberal Protestant thinkers discarded the traditional idea of miracles as narrated in the Bible. Instead, they emphasized the moral and religious transformation that Christianity brought to people's lives. Such liberal Protestant theologians were less concerned with the historical truth of the Bible and more concerned with its teachings on salvation.

CANONIZATION

In the Roman Catholic Church, canonization is the formal process for entering a name into the official list (canon) of recognized saints. The authority to declare a person a saint is reserved for the pope. Canonization imposes veneration of the saint upon the whole church. Prayers may be offered to the saint, who may then intercede with God on his devotee's behalf.

The first step toward canonization is beatification. All materials concerning a candidate's reputation (including information about miracles that he or she had performed) are investigated by two men appointed by the bishop. Based on this investigation, the pope may order the beatification. For a beatified saint to be considered for canonization, he or she must perform at least two authentic miracles on behalf of his or her regional devotees.

The early 20th century saw a return to a more traditional religious climate—one that was more willing to accept miracles as meaningful signs of God's salvation. This was due, in part, to new developments in science that questioned a rigid idea of causality.

Orthodox Jews, Christians, and Muslims still believe in the literal occurrence of the miracles recorded in their scriptures and traditions. Roman Catholics, in particular,

As part of his canonization, Pope Saint John Paul II (1920–2005) was found by a Vatican commission of medical doctors to be responsible for two cases of miraculous healing, thus making him eligible for sainthood.

believe miracles still occur. For them, miracles can be defined as a direct divine effect upon nature. A person who is officially recognized by the church as being very holy may be declared a saint. In most cases, part of this process, called canonization, involves the verification of miracles that are attributed to the person being considered for sainthood.

Over the years, many explanations have been offered for famous historical miracles. Some devout followers seek extreme scientific explanations for how the plagues in Egypt occurred or the Red Sea split. Ironically, such a scientific explanation would make these events no longer miracles but scientific possibilities. Despite scientific explanations, religious followers still find miraculous qualities in the timing of certain events or their seemingly undeserved occurrence.

CHAPTER FOUR

MIRACLES IN ARTS AND POPULAR CULTURE

B ecause of how important miracles have been to so many religions, they have been a frequent subject of the arts. Miracles are depicted in artwork, in literature, and in film. Because miracles are often understood through the subjective eyes of believers, their portrayal in the arts generally reflects individual religious beliefs.

IN PAINTINGS

In the Greco-Roman world, paintings often illustrated the feats of pagan gods. As early Judaism was a religion that disapproved of the visual depiction of biblical scenes and figures, illustration of the biblical miracles would not happen until Christian art more fully developed. This

Illuminated manuscripts often included illustrations of biblical scenes, including miracles. This illustration from the León Bible of 960 depicts Moses striking the rock, a biblical episode in which Moses's rod causes water to flow from a rock for the thirsty Israelites.

ILLUMINATED MANUSCRIPTS

One of the most popular sources of biblical illustrations was illuminated manuscripts. These were handwritten books decorated with gold or silver, brilliant colors, designs, and miniature pictures. During the Middle Ages, from about 500 to about 1500 CE, the Christian church was the only stable institution in western Europe. The monasteries alone kept culture and learning alive. Many monks were fine artists and craftsmen. The manuscripts they copied and decorated, called illuminated manuscripts, are the most beautiful examples of the period's art. The miracles recorded in both the Hebrew Bible and in the New Testament were a frequent subject of illuminated manuscripts. In 2007 the British Library published *Marvellous to Behold: Miracles in Medieval Manuscripts*, a collection of 117 such illustrations showing miracles.

began in the 3rd century CE. As early as the first half of the 3rd century, we begin to find stories from the Hebrew Bible alongside stories from the New Testament illustrated in paintings in the Roman Empire.

From the late 6th century, images became valued as a means of teaching Christian doctrine to those who could not read. Altarpieces and frescoes depicting scenes from the life of Jesus became popular. Early Christian art

Saint Zenobius Raises a Boy from the Dead, *tempera on panel, 1462, by Benozzo Gozzoli.*

particularly focused on depicting the miracles of Jesus. Late medieval and Renaissance art, in turn, focused on Jesus's humanity and role as a moral teacher. Still, paintings of the lives and works of miracle-working saints abound.

IN WRITINGS

The earliest writings about miracles were, of course, religious documents. Jewish, Christian, and Muslim theologians discussed the nature of miracles and whether particular ones had or had not truly occurred. In early Judaism, the tales of miracle workers were recorded in the Talmud. The two most notable are Honi the Circle Drawer (flourished 1st century BCE) and Hanina ben Dosa (flourished 1st century CE). In the Christian tradition, miracles are famously discussed by St. Thomas Aquinas in his 13th-century work *Summa contra Gentiles.* There he categorized miracles into three classes. Muslim theologian Al-Ghazali (1058–1111) discussed the nature of miracles in his monumental text *The Inconsistency of the Philosophers.*

In the early modern period, miracles would be reexamined through the lens of reason. Dutch-Jewish philosopher Baruch Spinoza (1632–77) wrote in his *Tractatus Theologico-Politicus* that all miracles have a cause, and believers simply ignore or don't look for one. In 1748 David Hume published *An Enquiry Concerning Human Understanding*, section ten of which is an

Baruch Spinoza.

essay titled "Of Miracles." Hume used probability to determine that miracles are highly unlikely (although not impossible).

Many 20th-century Christian thinkers tried to argue that miracles are rational. C. S. Lewis (1898–1963) is best known as the author of the series of books called The Chronicles of Narnia, but he also produced many writings on Christianity. Published in 1947, Lewis's *Miracles* puts forth his arguments in favor of divine intervention. Lewis sought to disprove naturalism, a belief that all beings and events are natural. Norman Geisler (1932–) and William Lane Craig (1949–) also wrote books defending miracles on a rationalist basis. Today, miracles are a common plot device in Christian fiction.

IN FILM & THEATER

With the rise of filmmaking in the 20th century, miracles have been depicted on the big screen. Cecil B. DeMille (1881–1959) was known for his grandiose productions. He directed *The Ten Commandments* (1923; remade in 1956), a screen portrayal of the biblical book of Exodus. Many of the miracles of the Hebrew Bible, including the plagues cast upon Egypt and the splitting of the Red Sea, were portrayed in the film. DeMille also directed *The King of Kings* (1927), a depiction of the life of Jesus.

The Greatest Story Ever Told is a 1965 epic film on the life of Jesus, from the Nativity to Resurrection.

A still from Cecil B. DeMille's The Ten Commandments *(1956), starring Charlton Heston (shown here) as the biblical prophet Moses.*

The film's high budget did not pay off; critics were divided in their reception to it. In 1977, Franco Zeffirelli (1923–) directed *Jesus of Nazareth*, a miniseries devoted to Jesus's life. An animated film about the life of Jesus, *The Miracle Maker,* was released in 2000.

Jesus's life has also been depicted on stage. Perhaps the most famous treatments are the rock opera *Jesus Christ Superstar* (1970) and *Godspell* (1971).

Actor Jeff Fenholt plays Jesus, surrounded in the above scene by disciples, in Andrew Lloyd Webber and Tim Rice's Jesus Christ Superstar *on October 6, 1971.*

The 1992 film *Leap of Faith* stars Steve Martin as a phony faith healer. The drama-comedy exposes some of the contemporary methods used to deceive believers into accepting miracles. The film does not discredit miracles outright but suggests they are not a product of human intervention.

MIRACLE PLAY

In the early Middle Ages a new type of play originated, one that typically depicted the life and miracles of Jesus Christ. In the 13th century miracle plays were taken from the hands of the clergy. By the latter part of the 14th century, they were acted almost entirely by members of guilds, or unions of craftsmen. These guilds went from street to street with large wagons, called pageants, on which they set up a stage with crude scenery. The Creation, Noah and the Flood, Adam and Eve, Abraham and Isaac, and other stories of the Old Testament were presented in addition to incidents in the life of Jesus Christ. Many plays also depicted the lives of the saints.

Most of these plays, which started as a means of religious instruction, became so vulgar that they were condemned by the church. After the 15th century they almost ceased to be given.

Miracles are extraordinary events with no natural explanation. While reason and science have often been used to discredit them, their long history and secure place in the arts and cultures continue to give miracles importance for all human beings. For some believers, miracles continue to happen on a regular basis. In either case, their impact is undeniable.

GLOSSARY

ALLAH God to followers of Islam.

BUDDHISM A religion of eastern and central Asia growing out of the teaching of Gautama Buddha.

CAUSALITY The relation between a cause and its effect or between regularly correlated events or phenomena.

DEFIANCE The act or an instance of defying or challenging.

DIVINATION The art or practice of using omens or magic powers to foretell the future.

EXODUS The second book of the Hebrew Bible.

GENESIS The first book of the Hebrew Bible.

HEBREW BIBLE Written account of the sacred law, prophets, and writings of the ancient people of Israel; the basis of the Old Testament, which is the first part of the Christian Bible.

INTERVENTION Interference with the outcome or course, especially of a condition or process (as to prevent harm or improve functioning).

MANNA Food that was miraculously supplied to the Israelites in the wilderness.

MESSIAH In Judaism, the expected king and deliverer of the Jews; in Christianity, Jesus Christ.

MYSTIC A person who tries to gain religious or spiritual knowledge through prayer and deep thought.

NEW TESTAMENT Record of the life and teachings of Jesus and his early followers; second part of the Christian Bible.

ORACLE A person (as a priestess of ancient Greece) through whom a deity is believed to speak.

PAGAN A follower of a religion with multiple gods (as in ancient Rome).

PHENOMENON A rare or important fact or event.

SHAMANISM A religious phenomenon centered on the shaman, a person believed to achieve various powers through trance or ecstatic religious experience.

THEOLOGIAN One who studies religion.

FOR FURTHER READING

Hand, David. *The Improbability Principle: Why Coincidences, Miracles, and Rare Events Happen Every Day.* New York, NY: Scientific American/Farrar, Straus and Giroux, 2014.

Hume, David, and Stephen Buckle, ed. *An Enquiry Concerning Human Understanding and Other Writings.* Cambridge, U.K.: Cambridge University Press, 2007.

Kushner, Lawrence. *The Book of Miracles: A Young Person's Guide to Jewish Spiritual Awareness.* 10th anniversary ed. Woodstock, VT: Jewish Lights Publishing, 1997.

Larsen, Carolyn. *Miracles of Jesus.* Cincinnati, OH: Standard Publishing, 2012.

Lewis, C. S. *Miracles.* London, U.K.: Collins, 2012.

Morgan, Ellen, and Stephen Marchesi. *Who Was Jesus?* New York, NY: Grosset & Dunlap, 2015.

Patai, Raphael, and Hayah Bar-Yitshak. *Enyclopedia of Jewish Folklore and Traditions.* Armonk, NY: M.E. Sharpe, 2013.

Pettis, Jeffrey B. *The Sleeper's Dream: Asclepius Ritual and Early Christian Discourse* (Gorgias Studies in Classical and Late Antiquity). Piscataway, NJ: Gorgias Press, 2015.

Philostratus and Christopher P. Jones, ed. *The Life of Apollonius of Tyana* (Loeb Classical Library). Cambridge, MA: Harvard University Press, 2005.

Shott, James R. *Moses* (Young Reader's Christian Library). Uhrichsville, OH: Barbour Publishing, 2013.

Watkins, Basil. *The Book of Saints: A Comprehensive Bibliographical Dictionary.* 8th ed. London, U.K.: Bloomsbury T&T Clark, 2016.

Weddle, David L. *Miracles: Wonder and Meaning in World Religions.* New York, NY: New York University Press, 2010.

Woodward, Kenneth L. *The Book of Miracles: The Meaning of the Miracle Stories in Christianity, Judaism, Buddhism, Hinduism and Islam.* New York, NY: Simon & Schuster, 2000.

WEBSITES

Because of the changing nature of Internet links, Rosen Publishing has developed an online list of websites related to the subject of this book. This site is updated regularly. Please use this link to access this list:

http://www.rosenlinks.com/UTP/miracle

INDEX